Our Church

on

Solid Ground

~

Documents for Preserving

Our Integrity and Unity

Our Church

on

Solid Ground

~

Documents for Preserving

Our Integrity and Unity

Christian Communicators Worldwide
Kansas City, Missouri

Scripture taken from The Holy Bible, New King James Version

For information regarding additional copies of
Our Church on Solid Ground, write:

Christian Communicators Worldwide
201 Main Suite #3
Parkville (Kansas City), MO 64152
USA

E-mail: info@CCWonline.org
Online orders: www.CCWonline.org

Cover design by Thomas Jones

Table of Contents

Introduction

If you were to attend church gatherings in Afghanistan, Botswana, Hong Kong, and New York City, all in one month, you would likely be amazed at the cultural diversity among Christians. There is beauty in this diversity that God Himself has created. However, in matters of doctrine and practice plainly set forth in the Bible, all Christians have an obligation to pursue like-mindedness.

This book contains three concise summaries of beliefs and practices which we believe are unambiguous in the Bible. First, the core doctrines of Christianity are arranged in *Holding Fast the Word of Life*, our statement of faith. Alongside this summary is an important tool entitled "How We Use Our Statement of Faith." Next, *The Fellowship of the Spirit* explains God's standard of conduct for the members of His church. The last section, *Restoring Those Who Fall*, details the biblical basics of church discipline, the primary means God has designed for securing the boundaries of Christian belief and behavior.

Many insist that churches will prosper only when certain biblical doctrines and practices are marginalized or refitted to mesh with the surrounding culture. In contrast, we are convinced that the local church will be strongest when biblical doctrines and practices are clearly defined and then faithfully upheld, despite the expectations of those around us and in humble submission to the Head of the church, our Lord Jesus Christ.

How We Use Our Statement of Faith

Churches have historically used confessions or statements of faith in order to summarize and clearly identify what they believe. Many historical confessions have been preserved, and are used by churches to this day. Instead of adopting an historical confession, we have chosen to use the following summary of biblical doctrine, entitled *Holding Fast the Word of Life*, as our statement of beliefs. Listed below are several important things you should understand about the purpose of our statement of faith, and about the way it will be used.

1. Our statement of faith will be a helpful introduction to the doctrines we will teach, giving you assurance that we will remain solidly biblical in our convictions. While we strongly believe that the doctrines set forth in our statement are an accurate summary of biblical truth, we do not require everyone joining our church to understand and affirm the statement at every point.

2. We may invite guest speakers who do not agree with every point of doctrine in our statement of faith. There are many faithful ministers of the Word who do not hold to the exact expression of our convictions. Though our statement will guide us in selecting those we choose for guest speaking, it will not preclude those who are in complete agreement in the most basic areas, while differing somewhat on secondary issues.

3. We *do* expect conformity to the statement of faith for our pastors, interns, and teachers—those most associated with the pastoral duty of teaching the truth. This does not imply that every teacher must have a thoroughly formulated understanding of every aspect of the statement. It does mean, however, that they are willing not to knowingly teach contrary to the established doctrine of the church while working out the finer points. Certain doctrines are so clear and so necessary that a teacher or potential leader would have no reason to be in confusion over them (e.g. the inerrancy of Scripture, the deity of Christ, the nature of saving faith, the sovereignty of God in electing, etc.). However, certain difficult points of doctrine may take even good students some time to work out (e.g. the extent of the atonement, the precise relationship between the covenants, etc.). Since any teaching is a pastoral extension, the pastor(s) will decide which points of theology, on a case by case basis, may remain suspended in the mind of a teacher or potential leader. Pains should be taken, however, to remove the confusion and to come to a solid conviction and doctrinal unity.

4. If a teacher comes to a conclusion contrary to the statement of faith, he is required to inform the pastor(s) about his conflicting belief. The pastor(s) will work with his concerns until there is unity in understanding. If an issue in the statement is found to be in error when compared with the Word of God, a correction will be made to the statement. If unity is unattainable, then the pastor(s) and the individual must fall back on the statement of faith as correct, until proven otherwise. In this case, the teacher will be asked to discontinue teaching until there is a better resolve. It is possible that at some point, a pastor or teacher may completely apostatize (i.e. disbelieve certain essential doctrines once held true). In that special case, church discipline is in order and all teaching responsibilities will be terminated.

5. Our statement of faith is subservient to the Scriptures. It should never be viewed as having an authority equal to that of the Bible. It is authoritative only in a limited sense, as far as it accurately reflects the meaning of Scripture. We view it and use it as a tool to promote, achieve, and maintain doctrinal understanding, purity, and harmony.

Holding Fast the Word of Life
Our Statement of Faith

Preface

The church is "the pillar and support of the truth" (1 Timothy 3:15). It is the responsibility of every member of the church to "contend earnestly for the faith which was once for all delivered to the saints" (Jude 3).

God's truth has always been questioned, attacked, and perverted. The Bible warns us that such deception will continue, and history has demonstrated the accuracy of these warnings. It is no wonder, then, that in our day, truth is rare while error is rampant.

We offer this statement of faith, not as something new or profound, not as a response to any single system of false doctrine, but rather as a simple and sincere attempt to proclaim and defend God's inerrant Word.

We pray that the reader, whether in agreement or disagreement, will emulate the fair-minded people of Berea who "searched the Scriptures daily to find out whether these things were so" (Acts 17:11).

Beware lest anyone cheat you through philosophy and empty deceit, according to the tradition of men, according to the basic principles of the world, and not according to Christ.
Colossians 2:8

Holding Fast the Word of Life
Our Statement of Faith

Be diligent to present yourself approved to God,
a worker who does not need to be ashamed,
rightly dividing the word of truth.

2 Timothy 2:15

1. The Holy Scripture

God has revealed all that is necessary for life and salvation in the sixty-six books of the Bible, which is the Word of God.[1] All Scripture is inerrant and infallible, transmitted through human authors by the inspiration of the Holy Spirit.[2] Scripture *alone**
is the final authority in all matters of doctrine and practice. The authority of Scripture is derived from its Author and not from the opinions of men.[3]

2. God and the Trinity

There is one true and living God[1] who exists in three eternally distinct persons:[2] the Father, the Son, and the Holy Spirit.[3] These three are one in being,[4] united in purpose,[5] and equally worthy of glory and adoration.[6] God is invisible, eternal, omni-present, almighty, all-knowing, unchanging, dependent upon none, sovereign, righteous, holy, just, gracious, loving, merciful, patient, and good.[7]

3. Creation

God created all that now exists in six days and from nothing, and it was all very good.[1] The Father, the Son, and the Holy Spirit acted together in the work of creation.[2] Out of all living things, only man was created in God's image. God granted him dominion over all lesser forms of life and over the earth itself.[3]

4. Providence

God orders and directs His universe in every detail.[1] Every event in nature and every human action and decision is according to His decree and purpose.[2] In God's infinite wisdom and power, all things work together for the benefit of His people,[3] and for His glory.[4]

5. The Fall and Its Effects

God made Adam perfect, holy, and upright,[1] appointing him representative and head of the human race.[2] He fell from his original righteousness into sin when he disobeyed God's command.[3] By his sinful act, Adam brought all people into a state of death and condemnation, passing to each one of them a corrupt sinful nature.[4]

6. Man's Inability

The Fall brought every man into a state of utter depravity, meaning every dimension of his being is distorted by sin.[1] Apart from the grace of God, fallen man treats sin as his master,[2] God as an enemy,[3] and the message of the cross as foolishness.[4] Until he is born again, he possesses neither the desire nor the ability to love God, to keep His laws, to understand the gospel, to repent of sin, or to trust in Christ.[5]

7. The Birth and Life of Christ

God sent His Son into the world to save His people from their sins.[1] Conceived of the Holy Spirit and born of the virgin Mary,[2] Jesus was and is both God and man.[3] He was tempted in all things yet without sin,[4] living the perfect life of righteousness on behalf of His people.[5]

8. The Death of Christ

Jesus died on the cross[1] as the perfect sacrifice for sin,[2] forever finishing the substitutionary work of atonement[3] for His people.[4]

9. The Resurrection of Christ

On the third day, Jesus rose bodily from the grave.[1] The resurrection affirms the deity and authority of Christ[2] and assures believers of their future bodily resurrection.[3]

10. The Ascension of Christ

Jesus ascended into heaven[1] to appear in the presence of God as our perpetual High Priest, presenting Himself as the only acceptable sacrifice for sin.[2] He is the one and only Mediator between God and men,[3] and Head of His church.[4] He intercedes forever on behalf of His people[5] and rules over all things for their sake.[6]

11. Election and Responsibility

Before the foundation of the world, God elected a great multitude of men and women to eternal life[1] as an act of His free grace *alone**. This election was in no way dependent upon His foresight of human faith, decision, works, or merit.[2] In the unsearchable realm of God's sovereign will,[3] all men remain responsible beings, subject to God's commands to repent and believe, and accountable to God for their rebellion, impenitence, and rejection of Christ.[4]

12. Calling and Regeneration

To accomplish God's redemptive purpose,[1] the Holy Spirit works effectively through the gospel of Christ,[2] regenerating elect sinners[3] and drawing them irresistibly to repentance and saving faith.[4]

13. Justification

The elect are declared righteous in the sight of God because of Christ's perfect life, His substitutionary death, and the imputation of His righteousness.[1] Justification can never be the reward or result of human works or merit,[2] nor does it grow out of an infusion of Christ's righteousness.[3] It is granted through faith *alone**[4] in the person and work of Christ *alone*.*[5]

14. Sanctification

According to God's purpose in predestination, the justified are progressively conformed to the image of Christ.[1] All true believers direct their will and affections toward this purpose,[2] putting to death the desires and deeds of the flesh[3] by the enabling power of the Holy Spirit[4] as God's Word is more fully understood and applied.[5] While sinless perfection will never be attained in this life,[6] it is a certainty in heaven.[7]

15. Perseverance

All who are chosen, called, regenerated, and justified shall persevere in faith and never finally fall away.[1] Perseverance is not a human accomplishment but a work of God through the indwelling presence of the Holy Spirit who creates, sustains, and nourishes a living, growing, transforming, and enduring faith in all true believers.[2]

16. The Church

A local church is a visible representation of the body of Christ and is under the authority of Christ alone.[1] Nevertheless, in every local church, qualified elders are appointed to serve Christ as they care for His body.[2] Qualified deacons are to assist the elders as needs arise.[3] Each member of the church is uniquely gifted by the Holy Spirit to edify the body.[4] A local church must recognize and fellowship with the universal body of Christ as represented in other true churches.[5]

17. Baptism

Baptism is the first act of Christian obedience.[1] True baptism is immersion in water,[2] symbolizing both the believer's union with Christ in His death, burial, and resurrection to new life,[3] and his cleansing from sin.[4] Baptism may only be administered to those who demonstrate repentance from sin and make a credible profession of faith in Christ.[5]

18. The Lord's Supper

Following their baptism, Christians may, and indeed, must regularly partake of the Lord's Supper.[1] By breaking and eating the bread and drinking the cup, believers commemorate the suffering and death of Jesus on the cross.[2] Through the Lord's Supper, they affirm and celebrate their oneness, their separation from the world, and their fellowship with Christ in the New Covenant.[3]

19. Evangelism

It is the calling of every local church to make disciples of all nations, baptizing them in the name of the Father, the Son, and the Holy Spirit, teaching them to obey all that Christ has commanded.[1] It is a priority in evangelism to unite new believers with local churches.[2]

20. The Return of Christ

The Lord Jesus Christ shall come again to raise the dead bodily, both righteous and unrighteous.[1] The justified shall enjoy everlasting life in the presence of God in heaven, while the unjustified shall eternally endure God's wrath in hell.[2]

21. The Old Covenant

The Old Covenant, with the Law of Moses as its core,[1] was revealed to the nation of Israel,[2] promising earthly blessings for obedience,[3] and threatening curses for disobedience.[4] The purpose of the Old Covenant was never to offer eternal life,[5] but rather to govern the life and worship of the Old Testament nation of Israel,[6] to reveal the extent of man's depravity,[7] and to foreshadow Christ and the New Covenant.[8]

22. The New Covenant

The New Covenant, established through the person and redemptive work of Christ,[1] provides eternal blessings which are acquired by grace through faith.[2] The Old Covenant was fulfilled in Christ, thus becoming obsolete.[3] God's final words of revelation, given through Christ and His New Testament apostles and prophets,[4] have become the authority concerning Christian conduct, and the interpretive lens through which the Old Testament must be understood and applied.[5]

23. The Glory of God

Christians must live for God's glory *alone**[1] through their awareness and enjoyment of His person,[2] submission to His authority,[3] and reliance upon His goodness.[4] In truth, all things that have or will transpire, serve to glorify God as their highest purpose.[5]

For of Him and through Him and to Him are all things, to whom be glory forever. Amen.

Romans 11:36

* The italicized use of the word "alone" at various places in our statement of faith indicates our affirmation of the five "solas" of the Protestant Reformation. For a further description of these important doctrines, see page 23.

The Five Solas

Imbedded in our statement of faith are the following five critical Christian doctrines. For centuries before the Protestant Reformation, these truths were largely neglected, even denied by most professing Christian leaders.

1. Sola Scriptura (Scripture *alone*)
The Bible *alone* teaches all that is necessary for our salvation from sin and is the standard by which all Christian behavior must be measured.

2. Sola Gratia (by Grace *alone*)
In salvation we are rescued from God's wrath by His grace *alone*. God's spontaneous and unmerited favor is granted through the calling and regenerating work of the Holy Spirit who releases us from our willful bondage to sin and enables us to repent and believe in Christ.

3. Sola Fide (through Faith *alone*)
Justification is by grace *alone* through faith *alone*. Justification can never be the reward or result of human works or merit, nor does it grow out of an infusion of Christ's righteousness.

4. Solus Christus (because of Christ *alone*)
Our salvation is accomplished by the mediatorial work of Jesus Christ *alone*. His sinless life and substitutionary death *alone* are sufficient for our justification and reconciliation to the Father.

5. Soli Deo Gloria (for the Glory of God *alone*)
God glorifies Himself in all that He does. Therefore we should acknowledge His highest purpose and live for His glory *alone*.

Scripture Proofs

1. The Holy Scriptures

(1) Psalm 119:9; Matthew 4:4; Acts 20:32; Romans 1:16; 1 Thessalonians 2:13; 1 Timothy 4:16; 2 Timothy 3:15-17; Hebrews 4:12; James 1:21; 2 Peter 1:2-4; 3:15-16
(2) Psalm 19:7-9; 119:160; Proverbs 30:5; John 17:17; 2 Timothy 3:16-17; 2 Peter 1:19-21
(3) Psalm 138:2; Proverbs 30:6; Galatians 1:8-9; 1 Timothy 1:3; 6:3-5, 20-21; 2 Timothy 3:16-17; 2 John 9-11

2. God and the Trinity

(1) Deuteronomy 4:39; Isaiah 44:6; Matthew 16:15-16
(2) Matthew 28:19; Titus 3:4-6; Matthew 3:16-17
(3) *The Father*: Matthew 3:16-17; 6:9; John 17:1, 5, 11, 21, 24-25; *The Son*: Matthew 1:23; 3:16-17; John 1:1, 14; 5:19-23; 8:58 (cf. Exodus 3:14); John 10:31-33; 17:1, 5, 11, 21, 25; Romans 9:5; Philippians 2:5-6; Colossians 2:9; Titus 2:13; 3:4, 6 (cf. Isaiah 43:11; 45:21); Hebrews 1:1-4; 2 Peter 1:1; *The Holy Spirit*: Matthew 1:18 (cf. Luke 1:35); John 14:16-17; Acts 5:3-4; Romans 8:9-11; 1 Corinthians 2:10-12; 12:11; Hebrews 10:15-17 (cf. Jeremiah 31:33-34)
(4) Genesis 1:26-27; 3:22-24; Deuteronomy 6:4; 1 Timothy 3:16
(5) Isaiah 42:1; 48:16; 61:1-3; Matthew 28:19; John 5:19, 30; 14:26; 2 Corinthians 13:14; Titus 3:4-6
(6) Matthew 12:31-32; John 5:23; 17:5; Hebrews 1:6; 10:29; Revelation 4:11 (cf. Psalm 104:30); Revelation 5:12-14
(7) *invisible*—John 1:18; 4:24; Colossians 1:15; 1 Timothy 1:17; 1 John 4:12; *eternal*— Genesis 21:33; Deuteronomy 33:27; Psalm 90:2; 1 Timothy 1:17;

omnipresent—Psalm 139:7-12; Proverbs 15:3 *almighty*—Psalm 62:11; 65:6; Isaiah 40:15, 28; Psalm 115:3; *all-knowing*—Psalm 147:5; Isaiah 40:13-14, 28; 66:18; Romans 16:27; *unchanging*—Numbers 23:19; Malachi 3:6; Hebrews 13:8; James 1:17; *dependent upon none*—Genesis 1:1; Acts 17:25; *sovereign*—1 Chronicles 29:11-12; Psalm 47:2; 115:3; Proverbs 21:1; Lamentations 3:37-38; Isaiah 46:9-11; John 19:10-11; Ephesians 1:11; 1 Timothy 6:15; *righteous*—Ezra 9:15; Nehemiah 9:8; Psalm 89:14; 92:15; John 17:25; Hebrews 1:8-9; *holy*—Leviticus 11:44; Psalm 99:3, 5, 9; Isaiah 6:3; Revelation 4:8; *just*—Psalm 89:14; Romans 3:26; 1 Peter 3:18; *gracious*—Exodus 34:6; Jonah 4:2; Ephesians 1:5-8; 2:4-7; 1 Peter 2:3; *loving*—John 3:16; Romans 5:8; Ephesians 2:4-5; 1 John 3:1; 4:8-10 (cf. Malachi 1:2-3; Romans 9:10-15; Hebrews 12:5-8); *merciful*—Exodus 34:6-7; Numbers 14:18; Psalm 136; Lamentations 3:22-23 (cf. Exodus 33:19; Romans 9:15); *patient*—Exodus 34:6-7; Numbers 14:18; Jonah 4:2; Romans 2:4; 9:22-23; 2 Peter 3:9; *good*—Exodus 34:6; Psalm 34:8; Luke 18:19

3. Creation

(1) Genesis 1; Exodus 20:11; 31:17; Acts 17:24; Romans 4:17; Hebrews 11:3; Revelation 4:11
(2) Genesis 1:1-2, 26-28; Psalm 33:6, 9; 104:30; Jeremiah 10:12-13; John 1:1-3; Colossians 1:15-17; Hebrews 1:2; 11:3
(3) Genesis 1:26-28; 9:6; Psalm 8:3-8; Colossians 3:10; James 3:9

4. Providence

(1) 1 Chronicles 29:11-12; Job 38:4-41; Proverbs 16:33; Isaiah 46:9-11; Romans 11:36; Ephesians 1:11; Acts 17:25, 28; Hebrews 1:3
(2) Exodus 4:21; 5:2; 7:2-5; 9:15-16 (cf. Romans 9:17-21); Proverbs 16:9; 21:1, Daniel 4:25, 35; Matthew 10:29; John 6:37-40; Acts 4:27-28; 13:48; Philippians 2:12-13

(3) Romans 8:28; Hebrews 12:5-11 (cf. Deuteronomy 8:15-16)

(4) Exodus 9:16 (cf. Exodus 7:3-5); Isaiah 60:21; Ezekiel 28:20-24; Romans 9:22-24; 11:33-36; Ephesians 1:3-6, 11-14

5. The Fall and Its Effects

(1) Genesis 1:26-31; Ecclesiastes 7:29
(2) Romans 5:12-19; 1 Corinthians 15:22
(3) Genesis 2:16-17; 3:1-24
(4)Genesis 6:12; Psalm 51:5; 58:3; Ecclesiastes 7:20; Romans 3:9-19, 23; 5:12, 18, 19; 6:23 (cf. James 1:14-15); 1 Corinthians 15:22

6. Man's Inability

(1) Genesis 6:5, 12; Jeremiah 17:9; Romans 1:28-32; 3:9-18; Titus 1:15
(2) Romans 6:16-22; Ephesians 2:1-3; Colossians 1:13; 2 Timothy 2:26; Titus 3:3
(3) Romans 5:10; 8:6-8; Colossians 1:21; James 4:4
(4) 1 Corinthians 1:18, 21; 2 Corinthians 2:15-16
(5) Jeremiah 13:23; John 3:3 (cf. Mark 4:10-12); John 3:19-20; 6:44, 65; 8:43, 45, 47; 14:17; 15:5; Romans 1:21; 3:9-18; 8:6-8; 1 Corinthians 2:14; 2 Corinthians 4:3-4; Ephesians 2:1; 4:17-19; Colossians 2:13; 2 Thessalonians 3:2 (cf. John 3:27; 1 Corinthians 4:7; Hebrews 11:6; 2 Peter 1:1)

7. The Birth and Life of Christ

(1) Matthew 1:21; John 1:29; 3:16-17; 1 John 3:5
(2) Isaiah 7:14; Matthew 1:18-23; Luke 1:26-35
(3) John 1:1, 14; 20:28-29; Romans 5:15, 18-19; 9:5; 1 Corinthians 15:47-49; Philippians 2:7-8; 1 Timothy 2:5; Titus 2:13; Hebrews 1:8; 2:17
(4) Isaiah 53:9; Matthew 4:1-11; John 8:46; Hebrews 4:15; 7:26-28; 1 Peter 2:17-19; 1 John 3:5
(5) 2 Corinthians 5:21; Galatians 4:4-5

8. The Death of Christ

(1) Mark 15:37, 44-45; 1 Corinthians 15:3-4; Revelation 1:18; Romans 10:9
(2) 2 Corinthians 5:21; Hebrews 2:10; 9:9-14; 10:10-14
(3) John 19:28-30; Romans 3:23-25; 2 Corinthians 5:18-21; Hebrews 7:23-27; 1 John 2:2; 4:10
(4) John 10:14-16; 15:12-14; Acts 20:28; Romans 8:28-34; Ephesians 5:25; Hebrews 10:12-14

9. The Resurrection of Christ

(1) Matthew 28:5-7; Luke 24:5-8, 39, 42-43
(2) Romans 1:4; John 2:19-21 (cf. 5:21, 26); Acts 2:29-36; 17:31; Ephesians 1:20-22; Philippians 2:8-11;
(3) Romans 6:5-9; 1 Corinthians 6:14; 15:12-19, 22; 2 Corinthians 4:14; Philippians 3:20-21

10. The Ascension of Christ

(1) Luke 24:51; Acts 1:9-11
(2) Hebrews 7:23-27; 9:11-14, 24; 10:4, 10-14
(3) 1 Timothy 2:5; Hebrews 8:6; 9:15; 12:24
(4) Matthew 16:16-18; Ephesians 1:22; 5:23; Colossians 1:18
(5) Isaiah 53:12; Romans 8:34; Hebrews 7:23-25; 1 John 2:1
(6) 1 Corinthians 15:24-26; Ephesians 1:18-23; Philippians 2:9-11

11. Election and Responsibility

(1) John 6:37-39; 10:14-16; 17:2; Acts 13:48; Romans 8:28-30; Ephesians 1:3-6, 11-12; 2 Thessalonians 2:13
(2) Romans 9:10-16; 11:5-10; Ephesians 2:8; Philippians 1:29; 2 Timothy 1:9
(3) Deuteronomy 29:29; Isaiah 55:8-9; Romans 11:33-34; 1 Corinthians 2:16
(4) Matthew 25:31-46; Mark 1:15; John 3:36; 6:37; Acts 17:30-31; Romans 1:18-21; 2:4-5; 9:19-22; 2 Thessalonians 1:5-10

12. Calling and Regeneration

(1) Isaiah 55:10-11; Ezekiel 34:11-13, 16 (cf. Luke 19:10); Matthew 1:21; 2 Thessalonians 2:13
(2) Romans 1:16; 10:14-17; 1 Corinthians 1:21; 1 Peter 1:23-25; 1 Thessalonians 1:4-5; 2 Thessalonians 2:14
(3) Deuteronomy 30:6; Jeremiah 31:33; Ezekiel 36:26-27; John 1:13; 3:3-8; 1 Corinthians 6:11; 2 Corinthians 4:6; Ephesians 2:10; Titus 3:5; James 1:18
(4) John 6:37, 44-45, 65; 10:16; Acts 2:39; Romans 8:30; 1 Corinthians 1:26-29; Hebrews 9:15

13. Justification

(1) Isaiah 53:11; Romans 4:5-8, 11, 16, 20-25; 2 Corinthians 5:21; 8:9; 1 Peter 1:18-19
(2) Romans 3:20-21, 27-28; 4:1-5; 10:1-4; Galatians 2:15-16; 20-21; 3:10-14; Titus 3:4-7
(3) Romans 4:1-8; 5:12-19; Hebrews 10:14
(4) Genesis 15:6; John 1:11-12; Romans 1:17; 3:20, 26-28; 4:5, 20-24; 5:1; Galatians 2:15-16, 20-21; 3:2-3, 5-9, 11-13; 5:1-6; Ephesians 2:8-9; Philippians 3:9
(5) John 3:14-18, 36; 14:6; Acts 4:12; 2 John 9; 1 Corinthians 16:22

14. Sanctification

(1) Proverbs 4:18; Romans 8:29; 2 Corinthians 3:18; 4:16; 1 Thessalonians 3:10; 5:23-24
(2) Matthew 5:6; 7:21; John 14:15, 21; Hebrews 12:14; James 2:14-26; 2 Peter 1:5-11; 1 John 2:3-6; 3:3; 3 John 11
(3) Romans 8:13; Galatians 5:24; Philippians 3:14; Colossians 3:1-11
(4) Ezekiel 36:27; Romans 8:8-14; Philippians 2:13
(5) Psalm 1:1-3; 19:7-8; 119:9, 11, 133; Proverbs 2:1-9; John 17:17; Acts 20:32; Ephesians 5:26; 1 Thessalonians 2:13; 2 Timothy 3:15-17; James 1:21-25; 1 Peter 2:1-3

(6) Proverbs 20:9; Ecclesiastes 7:20; Philippians 3:12-14; James 3:2; 1 John 1:8,10

(7) 1 Corinthians 13:9-12; Ephesians 5:27; Philippians 1:6; 1 Thessalonians 5:24; Hebrews 12:1-2; 1 John 3:2; Jude 24; Revelation 21:27

15. Perseverance

(1) John 5:24; 10:27-29; Romans 8:1-2; 28-39; 1 Thessalonians 5:23-24; Hebrews 3:14; 1 Peter 1:5; 1 John 2:19

(2) Romans 1:16-17; 2 Corinthians 3:18; Galatians 2:20; Philippians 2:13; 1 Thessalonians 5:23-24; 2 Timothy 1:12; 1 Peter 1:3-5; Jude 24

16. The Church

(1) 1 Corinthians 3:9; 12:12-14, 27; 1 Peter 2:4-5; Matthew 16:16-18; Ephesians 1:22-23; 5:23-24a

(2) Acts 20:17,28; 1 Timothy 3:1-7; Titus 1:5-9; Hebrews 13:17; 1 Peter 5:2-4

(3) Acts 6:1-4; 1 Timothy 3:8-13

(4) Romans 12:3-8; 1 Corinthians 12:7,11; 14:12, 26, Ephesians 4:11-16; 1 Peter 4:10-11

(5) Ecclesiastes 4:9-12; Galatians 3:26 (cf. 1:2); 2 Corinthians 11:28; Colossians 4:16

17. Baptism

(1) Matthew 28:19; Mark 16:16; Acts 2:38, 41; 8:36-38; 9:18; 10:47-48; 16:14-15, 31-34; 18:8

(2) Matthew 3:16; Mark 1:10; John 3:23; Acts 8:36-38

(3) Acts 19:3-5; Romans 6:3-6; Galatians 2:20; Colossians 2:11-14

(4) Acts 2:38; 22:16; 1 Corinthians 6:11; Titus 3:5; Hebrews 10:22

(5) Matthew 28:19; Acts 2:38; 16:31-34

18. The Lord's Supper

(1) Luke 22:19; 1 Corinthians 11:24-25
(2) Luke 22:19-20; 1 Corinthians 11:26
(3) Matthew 26:27-28; Luke 22:20; Acts 2:42; 1 Corinthians 10:16-17,21

19. Evangelism

(1) Psalm 86:9; Malachi 1:11; Matthew 9:36-38; 28:19-20; Acts 1:8; 2 Corinthians 5:18-20; Revelation 5:9
(2) Acts 20:28 (cf. Ezekiel 34:11-14); Matthew 16:18; Acts 2:47; 1 Corinthians 3:9; Ephesians 4:14-16; 1 Peter 2:5

20. The Return of Christ

(1) John 5:28-29; 14:3; Acts 1:11; 1 Corinthians 15:51-57; 1 Thessalonians 4:13-18; Hebrews 9:28
(2) Matthew 25:31-46; 2 Thessalonians 1:6-9; Hebrews 9:27-28; Revelation 20:11-21:8; 22:3-5, 14-15

21. The Old Covenant

(1) Exodus 20:1-23:33 (cf. 24:3-4, 7, 12; 34:27-28; Deuteronomy 4:13-14); John 1:17; Acts 15:5 (cf. v. 10); Hebrews 10:28
(2) Deuteronomy 4:7-8; Romans 3:1-2; Galatians 2:14b
(3) Deuteronomy 7:12-24; 11:13-15, 26-29; 28:1-14
(4) Deuteronomy 11:16-17, 26-29; 28:15-68
(5) John 5:39-40; Romans 3:19-22; 8:3; 10:1-4; Galatians 2:16, 21; 3:19-23; Hebrews 7:18-19
(6) Deuteronomy 4:5-6, 14; 6:1-3; 10:12-13
(7) Romans 3:20; 5:20; 7:7-13; Galatians 3:19
(8) Deuteronomy 18:15-19 (cf. Acts 3:14-24; 7:37, 51-53); Luke 24:44; John 5:39; Colossians 2:16-17; Hebrews 9:6-14, 23-24; 10:1; 13:11-12

22. The New Covenant

(1) Luke 22:20; 1 Corinthians 5:7; Hebrews 7:22; 8:6; 9:11-26; 13:20

(2) Romans 4:1-25; 6:14; Ephesians 2:8-9; Titus 3:4-7

(3) Matthew 5:17-20; Romans 7:4, 6; 10:4; 2 Corinthians 3:2-11; Galatians 3:24-25; 4:21-31; Ephesians 2:14-16; Colossians 2:13-14; Hebrews 7:11-12, 18-19, 22; 8:1-13; 10:9b

(4) John 1:17-18; 13:34-35; Ephesians 2:19-20; 3:4-5 (cf. John 16:12-14)

(5) Deuteronomy 18:15-19 (cf. John 12:49); Matthew 5:22, 28, 32, 34, 39, 44; 28:20a; John 13:34-35; 14:15, 21, 23; 15:10, 14; Romans 14:5-6; 1 Corinthians 9:21; Colossians 2:16-17 (cf. 2 Chronicles 2:4; 8:12-13; 31:3); Colossians 3:15-17; Hebrews 7:12; 10:28-29 (cf. Deuteronomy 18:19; John 12:47-50)

23. The Glory of God

(1) Leviticus 10:3; Matthew 5:16; 1 Corinthians 10:31; Philippians 1:9-11; 1 Peter 4:11

(2) Psalm 23:4; 46:1; 139:7-10, 17-18; Proverbs 15:3; Jeremiah 16:17; Matthew 28:20; Hebrews 13:5-6

(3) 1 Samuel 15:22-23; Ecclesiastes 12:13-14; Micah 6:8; John 15:14-16 (cf. John 15:8; Ephesians 2:10); Hebrews 12:28-29

(4) Psalm 23; 18:1-3; 34:7-10; Isaiah 41:10; Habakkuk 3:17-19; Matthew 6:25-32; Luke 11:11-13; Acts 17:24-25, 28; 2 Corinthians 1:3-4; Philippians 4:6-7; James 1:17

(5) Psalm 46:10; 86:9; Malachi 1:11; Romans 11:36; Ephesians 1:3-14; 3:20-21

The Fellowship of the Spirit
Our Membership Agreement

As a follower of Jesus Christ, I joyfully and thoughtfully enter into a bond of mutual edification,[1] fellowship,[2] and accountability[3] with the other members of this body. I have repented of my sin,[4] trusted in Christ as my Savior and Lord,[5] and been baptized as a true believer.[6]

I will faithfully participate with this church in worship, prayer, study, fellowship, and the ordinances of baptism and communion.[7] I will use my spiritual gifts for the common good.[8] Through my involvement, and even sacrifice, I will seek to illustrate to my family and a watching world the immense significance of life in the body of Christ.[9]

In addition to the regular meetings of the church and in the spirit of a true disciple of Christ, I will diligently train myself and my family in the discipline and instruction of the Lord, seeking to develop Christian character, knowledge, and skills.[10]

I will work toward doctrinal unity with a humble and teachable spirit.[11] For this reason, I am willing to be taught according to the statement of faith which this church believes to be an accurate summary of biblical truth.[12] Where there is disagreement or a lack of understanding regarding doctrinal convictions, I assume the liberty to ask questions and engage in edifying discussion. I will reject all heretical beliefs and practices, using Scripture as the final authority.[13]

I will accept and fellowship with all members, regardless of race, gender, background, social status, or level of education, since all are of equal value in Christ.[14]

I will pursue peace with all people, especially with other believers, always being slow to take offense and eager to reconcile.[15] I will shun gossip and divisive words, knowing that they are destructive to Christian fellowship.[16]

I will seek to live a life that is above reproach. I will be just and honest in my dealings and faithful in my responsibilities and commitments. I will abide by the standards of sexual purity and ethical integrity as taught in the Bible.[17]

I will seek the preservation of marriage, knowing that God hates divorce, and I will submit to biblical regulations regarding divorce and remarriage.[18]

I will watch over the other members in love as they watch over me.[19] I will remember them in prayer,[20] help them in sickness and distress,[21] promote their spiritual growth,[22] restrain them from sin,[23] and stir them up to love and good deeds.[24]

I will submit to the church's discipline upon myself and lovingly assume my responsibility to participate in the discipline of other members, as taught in Scripture.[25] If I am offended in connection with a disciplinary matter, I will seek resolution within the church. I will never initiate or pursue civil legal action against the church or any other Christian.[26]

I will contribute cheerfully and regularly to this church for its general ministry and expenses, the relief of the poor, the cause of reformation and revival, and the spread of the Gospel throughout the world. I will dedicate myself, my money, and my possessions to the cause of Christ as a faithful steward, avoiding all forms of greed.[27]

I will seek the salvation of my family, friends, neighbors, co-workers, acquaintances, and people of all nations.[28]

I promise to remain faithful to this church in membership. I will consult with the pastor(s) in advance if I sense that God is directing me elsewhere. If I must leave, I will unite with another true church.[29]

In summary, I will love the Lord my God with all my heart, soul, mind, and strength, and I will love others as Christ loves me.[30]

I will not allow my weaknesses and failures to deter me from my intention to abide by these Christian standards. I will pursue holiness through genuine repentance and persevering faith in the One to whom I owe all obedience for time and eternity, the Lord Jesus Christ.[31]

Scripture Proofs

(1) Romans 14:19; 1 Corinthians 12:7; 14:26; Ephesians 4:16, 29; 1 Thessalonians 5:11

(2) Acts 2:42; 1 Corinthians 1:9; 2 Corinthians 13:14; Ephesians 4:1-3; Philippians 2:1-4

(3) Proverbs 27:17; Matthew 18:15-17; Galatians 6:1; 2 Thessalonians 3:6,14-15; James 5:16; 2 John 8

(4) Matthew 4:17; Mark 1:15; Luke 13:1-5; Acts 2:38; 17:30; 26:20; 2 Corinthians 7:10

(5) John 3:16; Acts 4:12; 16:30-31; Romans 10:9-10

(6) Matthew 28:19; Acts 2:38; 8:36-38; 10:47-48

(7) Matthew 28:19; Luke 22:14-20; Acts 2:41-47; 1 Corinthians 11:23-26; Hebrews 10:24-25

(8) Romans 12:3-8; 1 Corinthians 12:4-7,18-27; Ephesians 4:11-16

(9) Matthew 6:19-21, 24-26; 16:24; Hebrews 10:24-25; James 4:1-5; 1 Peter 2:9-10; 1 John 2:15-17

(10) Deuteronomy 6:4-7; Proverbs 22:6; Ephesians 6:4; 1 Timothy 4:7; Hebrews 5:13-14; 1 Peter 2:1-3; 2 Peter 1:5-11; 3:17-18

(11) Psalm 133:1; Romans 15:5-6; 1 Corinthians 1:10; 2 Corinthians 13:11; Ephesians 4:1-6; Philippians 2:2

(12) Ephesians 4:11-14; 1 Timothy 4:16; Titus 1:9; 2:1; Hebrews 13:17; James 3:1

(13) Isaiah 8:20; Acts 17:11; 2 Corinthians 11:3-4; Galatians 1:6-9; 1 Thessalonians 5:21; 1 Timothy 1:3-4; 3:15; 6:3-5,20-21; 2 Timothy 2:15-18; 4:3-4; Hebrews 13:8-9; 2 John 9-11; Jude 3

(14) Romans 10:12; Galatians 3:26-28; James 2:1-5

(15) Matthew 5:23-24; Romans 12:18; 14:19; 1 Corinthians 13:4-7; Colossians 3:12-15; Hebrews 12:14; James 1:19-20

(16) Proverbs 6:16-19; 10:19; Romans 16:17; Ephesians 4:29,31; 1 Timothy 5:13; Titus 3:10-11; James 3:6-10

(17) Proverbs 10:9; Micah 6:8; Matthew 5:16, 37; Luke 16:10; 1 Corinthians 6:18; 2 Corinthians 6:3; Galatians 5:22; Ephesians 4:25; 1 Thessalonians 4:3-7; Titus 2:6-8; Hebrews 13:4
(18) Malachi 2:16; Matthew 5:31-32; 19:3-9; Mark 10:2-12; Luke 16:18; 1 Corinthians 7
(19) 1 Corinthians 10:24; Galatians 6:1-2,10; Philippians 2:4
(20) 2 Corinthians 1:11; Ephesians 6:18; Philippians 1:19; 1 Thessalonians 5:25; James 5:14-16
(21) Matthew 25:34-40; Romans 12:13,15; Galatians 6:2,10; Philippians 4:14; 1 John 3:16-18
(22) Titus 2:1-15; Hebrews 5:12-14; 2 Peter 3:17-18
(23) Proverbs 24:11; Galatians 6:1; 1 Timothy 5:20; James 5:19-20
(24) Ephesians 2:10; Titus 2:1-10; 3:8,14; Hebrews 10:24; 13:16
(25) Matthew 18:15-17; 1 Corinthians 5; 2 Thessalonians 3:6,14-15; 1 Timothy 5:20
(26) 1 Corinthians 6:1-8
(27) Malachi 3:8-10; 2 Corinthians 8:1-7; 9:6-7; Philippians 4:18
(28) Matthew 9:36-38; 28:18-20; Romans 10:14-15; 1 Corinthians 9:19-22; 2 Corinthians 5:18-20; 1 Peter 3:15
(29) Proverbs 3:5-6; 11:14; 12:15; 15:22; 18:1; 19:20; 20:18; 24:6; 1 Corinthians 12:18; Philippians 2:3-4; Hebrews 10:24
(30) Mark 12:28-31; John 13:34-35; 1 Corinthians 13:1-3; 1 John 3:16-19; 4:7-21
(31) Matthew 5:6; Philippians 3:12-14; Hebrews 12:1-4; 1 Peter 1:14-19

Restoring Those Who Fall

Our Statement Regarding Church Discipline

Church discipline is one of the primary means God uses to correct and restore His children when they fall into sin. It is also one way in which He maintains the unity, purity, integrity, and reputation of the church. Through private or public instruction, warning, counsel, or rebuke, and in some cases even social avoidance or expulsion from membership, God corrects his disobedient children or removes those who are not truly His. Christ Himself declared the church to be heaven's instrument in carrying out this difficult but necessary function (Matthew 18:15-20).

The purpose of this statement is to define, in general terms, five classes of sinful behavior for which church discipline may be necessary, and to explain how the Bible tells us to respond to each.[1] We must not assume, however, that every situation will fall neatly into a single category. Disciplinary matters are often confusing combinations or variations of these general classes, making the proper course of action difficult to determine. For this reason, the church must carry out discipline with prayer, diligent application of Scripture, and reliance upon the Spirit of God.

1. Minor Faults

Minor faults are attitudes and actions such as rudeness, impatience, grumbling, complaining, negativity, pettiness, boasting, irritability, speaking too much or when inappropriate, lack of trust, worry, timidity, selfishness, etc. They are minor sins *by comparison*, but are nevertheless contrary to biblical instructions to be considerate, patient, content, always thankful, always rejoicing, forbearing, humble, slow to anger, slow to speak, trusting, bold, selfless, etc.

We are permitted, and actually encouraged to overlook most minor faults rather than resorting to discipline (Proverbs 10:12; 19:11; Romans 15:1; 1 Peter 4:8). Should a minor fault be thought serious enough to require private counsel, we should be particularly careful to apply Christ's words about removing the "speck" from our brother's eye while a "plank" is in our own (Matthew 7:1-5). Only if a minor fault is repeated so consistently or in such a disruptive manner that it causes harm to the church should any measure(s) be taken beyond private instruction, warning, or rebuke.

2. Unverifiable Sins

Whether minor or serious, unverifiable sins are offenses that are known to *only one member* besides the offender(s). Additionally, they are matters in which *no evidence* could be brought forth as proof. For example: insulting words spoken in private, physical assault or theft where no physical or circumstantial evidence exists, breach of a private verbal contract, private awareness of another member's illicit behavior, etc.

In such cases, it may be necessary for the offended person or lone witness to rebuke the offender privately. But if private rebuke is unsuccessful and the offender is not willing to admit his sin to others, no further church action may be taken. The matter must be left with God; it should not be revealed to anyone else (Matthew 18:16, cf. Deuteronomy 19:15; Proverbs 25:8-10).

(Note: Exceptions to this rule include the reporting of criminal offenses to the proper authorities when necessary or required by law, and/or warning any individuals who are endangered by the offender. Even in these cases, however, unnecessary publicity among church members should be avoided.)

3. Personal Offenses

Personal offenses are offenses between two Christians—more specifically, two members of the same church. Personal offenses could be defined as "any sinful behavior by one member that causes harm to another." For example: insults, slander, breach of personal trust or contract, physical or sexual abuse, adultery, physical assault, theft, vandalism, etc. In these situations, the offended person must closely follow Matthew 18:15-17:

◆   He must first meet with the offender in private, explain his offense to him, and seek his repentance (Matthew 18:15).

◆   If the offender remains unrepentant, the offended person must be cautious before taking additional measures. If the offense is unverifiable (as defined above) or not significant enough to bring before the whole church, it should not be pursued further.

◆   If the offense is significant and verifiable, a meeting should be arranged (a mini trial, as described in 1 Corinthians 6:1-8), during which the offended person can present his case to the offender in the presence of one or two other members (Matthew 18:16). These should either be witnesses to the offense, or mature, discerning members who are able to evaluate evidence and testimony, question both parties effectively, determine guilt or responsibility, and offer appropriate biblical counsel.

◆   If the offender remains unrepentant even after his guilt has been proven before witnesses, the matter must be told to the general membership of the church at another meeting (Matthew 18:17). If the offender is present, the elder(s) should rebuke him publicly and implore him to confess and repent. If he is absent, the matter should still be revealed to the church (in appropriately limited detail, of course). In either case, the members of the church should be encouraged to make personal efforts to persuade him to repent. A date should be set for a final meeting, during which the matter will be brought to conclusion. The offender must be notified regarding this meeting (either in person or via certified mail) and encouraged to attend in the hope that he will make a public confession. (Note: Because the offender's guilt was established at the "mini-trial," no opportunity will ordinarily be given at these subsequent meetings for him to debate the matter or defend himself publicly.)

◆ At the final meeting, the offender (if present) will be offered a final opportunity to repent and be restored. Regarding a publicly known offense, repentance would begin with a public confession. If he remains unrepentant or is not present, he will be considered an unbeliever and expelled from membership (Matthew 18:17).

◆ Even if the offender repents at some point prior to expulsion from membership, restitution and/or other remedial actions may be necessary, as determined by the elders (i.e. mandated accountability, removal from church office, counseling, etc.).

4. Public Disobedience

Public disobedience describes sinful behavior that causes harm to the unity, doctrinal integrity, purity, or reputation of the church as a whole. This category would include false teaching, divisiveness, contentions, gossip, slander of the church or its leaders, insubordination, sexual immorality, drunkenness, covetousness, theft, dishonesty, outbursts of anger or fighting, foul language, willful failure to provide, wrongful divorce or remarriage, breach of public trust or contract, etc. The goals of church discipline in these situations are two:

1. to protect and preserve the unity, doctrinal integrity, purity, and reputation of the church (Acts 20:28-31; Hebrews 12:14-16)

2. to identify those who begin to commit these types of sins, employ various biblical measures to call them to repentance, and restore them when possible (Galatians 6:1; James 5:19-20).

Unlike the singularity and clarity of the instructions for resolving personal offenses (Matthew 18:15-17), the instructions for dealing with acts of public disobedience are much more varied. Especially here, we must pause, pray, seek wise counsel, and apply the Scriptures carefully, considering each situation to be unique.

The following is a general representation of the range of biblical measures we have been given to deal with public disobedience. Not every measure listed here will be appropriate for every situation. We have listed them in order of severity, from the most gentle or subtle to the most direct, but this should not be construed to mean that they must be applied in this order in every case.

• **Be watchful. Be on guard against offenses** (Acts 20:28-31; Hebrews 12:14-16; etc.). We should not aggressively hunt for offenses or opportunities to enact discipline (Matthew 13:28-30), but we must be vigilant, ready to address sinful behavior when it becomes known.

- **Note those who are offending and watch them closely** (Romans 16:17; 2 Timothy 3:1-5; 4:14-15). This is particularly the responsibility of the elders who are the shepherds of the flock. We are warned in the New Testament that there will be some who profess to be Christians who will seek to harm the church (Acts 20:30; 2 Peter 2:1-3). A person who begins to teach contrary to sound doctrine, is divisive or insubordinate, or seeks to exalt himself (i.e. 3 John 9-10), may be a "wolf in sheep's clothing" and must be watched carefully in order to protect the true sheep.

- **Correct through teaching** (2 Timothy 2:24-26; Titus 1:9). The Word of God is powerful and effective. In all cases, especially when more direct or severe measures are not immediately necessary, elders and other teachers must address disobedience by applying the Scriptures humbly, gently, patiently, and convincingly (also see 2 Timothy 3:16-4:2).

- **Plead with the offender(s)** (1 Corinthians 1:10-11; Philippians 4:2-3). Paul pleaded with the Corinthian church as a group, and with Euodia and Syntyche as individual Christians in Philippi, imploring them to stop being divisive or contentious. In both situations, his pleas, which were in the form of open letters to the churches, also served as gentle public rebukes.

- **Warn them of consequences** (1 Thessalonians 5:14; Titus 3:10-11). Unruly or disobedient Christians who have not responded to gentle or subtle disciplinary measures are exposing themselves to public rebuke, social avoidance, or even expulsion from the church. Warn them of these embarrassing and painful consequences. Warn them most seriously of the day when they will stand before the Lord Jesus to be judged according to their deeds (2 Corinthians 5:9-11).

+ **Rebuke them** (Galatians 2:11-14; 1 Timothy 5:20; Titus 1:13; 2:15). The prospect of being publicly rebuked should be a powerful deterrent to sinful behavior, both for the one rebuked, and for others who witness the rebuke. Public rebuke also serves the purpose of public teaching by identifying and exposing the nature of error (Ephesians 5:8-13).

+ **Silence them** (Titus 1:10-11). Paul insisted that false teachers and divisive people "must be silenced," and his implication was that the *leaders* of the church should make every effort to silence them. This could be accomplished through private warning, public rebuke and exposure of error, administrative removal from a teaching role, etc.

+ **Shame them through social avoidance** (2 Thessalonians 3:6,14-15). Demonstrate to them that their behavior is neither compatible with the Christian standard nor acceptable among the church, by excluding them from all fellowship *without* expelling them from membership. (Note: This type of brotherly exclusion is rare in the New Testament. It is most likely found only in 2 Thessalonians chapter 3, where the offense was idleness and unruliness due to misguided views about the nearness of the second coming of Christ. It is possibly seen in 2 Corinthians 2:5-8 as well, but the reasons for exclusion in that case are unknown.

The reference in Romans 16:17 is almost certainly to outsiders, not members of the church.).

These measures are all intended to correct and restore, and to maintain unity and purity. They are to be applied while there is still hope for repentance. None of them are as severe as expulsion from membership, which is the subject of the next section. It is possible that there may not be time to accomplish these measures before an offender becomes a divisive influence in the church. In such cases, he must be excluded from membership after one or two admonitions (Titus 3:10).

5. Insufferable Wickedness

Insufferable wickedness refers to situations where there is only one proper course of action—expulsion from membership. There are three types of offenders whose behavior should be considered insufferable, and who must be expelled:

Unrepentant personal offenders—those who have refused to acknowledge their sin and repent, even after public rebuke and exhortation from the entire church (Matthew 18:17).

Gross offenders—those who commit even a single sin that is so abhorrent, shameful, or notorious that the reputation of Christ and the church is imperiled if they are not immediately expelled (1 Corinthians 5:1,5,13).

Offenders who are known by their wickedness—professing Christians who are known publicly for such sins as heresy, apostasy, divisiveness, sexual immorality, drunkenness, covetousness,[2] etc. Their sinful lifestyle makes them indistinguishable from unbelievers. In others words, they are so characterized by false beliefs, false teaching, destructive motives, worldly affections, or immoral living that they cannot, by definition, be considered Christians (1 Corinthians 5:11-13; 6:9-10; Galatians 5:19-21; Titus 1:16; 1 John 1:5-6; 2:3-4; 3:9-10; 2 John 9-11).

In these situations, all that is necessary before expulsion is the establishment of the facts. We must notice that in 1 Corinthians chapter 5, Paul did not instruct the church to first warn the incestuous man or seek his repentance. No command was given to rebuke him, publicly or privately, before casting him out. With the man's gross immorality well-known to all, Paul told them to immediately expel him from the church (1 Corinthians 5:5,13). In verse 11 of the same chapter, Paul lists other types of offenders who must be treated in the same way (Also see 1 Timothy 1:20 and Titus 3:10-11). Even if sorrow is expressed by the offender at this point, expulsion is still necessary in order to maintain the reputation of Christ and the church.

Additional Considerations:

1. The desired result of church discipline is always repentance and the restoration of the offender. Our private and public disciplinary measures should always be undertaken in a spirit of love, gentleness, and humility as we seek to bring about this positive end (Galatians 6:1-2). When restoration does not occur and expulsion becomes necessary, we are glad to see the purity of Christ and the church upheld, but we should be grieved, individually and corporately, that one with whom we shared fellowship has become known to us as an unbeliever.

2. Genuine repentance consists of more than outward sorrow and tears (2 Corinthians 7:9-11). It becomes evident when the offender is willing not only to leave his sin, but also to confess it to all who are affected by it (even to the general membership of the church if necessary, as determined by the elders), and to make restitution when appropriate.

3. When a member is expelled or socially excluded, he or she may not attend any gathering of the church, unless it is with the permission of the elders and for the purpose of public confession. Members who have any necessary continuing association with an expelled person must not participate with him or her in any shared activity that might be construed as Christian fellowship (2 Corinthians 6:14-17; Ephesians 5:11). The manner of such association must also never imply approval of the offender's behavior and/or condemnation of the disciplinary action taken by the church (Proverbs 17:15).

4. In the case of a member who was expelled, restoration will be considered with great caution, and then only after the membership process is repeated in its entirety. Depending upon the nature of the offense, a restored member may have become disqualified for biblical offices within the church (i.e. elder or deacon) due to a tarnished reputation, issues regarding marriage and divorce, and/or an obvious weakness in a particular area (1 Timothy 3:2-3,7,10; Titus 1:6-8; 1 Peter 5:3).

5. Disciplinary matters should be addressed promptly upon discovery of the sin. Unnecessary delay is unprofitable since it permits the perpetuation of the sin, maintains an unhealthy tension within the church, and creates the perception of apathy regarding sinful behavior.

6. If an offending member leaves our church after initial disciplinary action begins but prior to expulsion from membership, the matter will still be brought to conclusion (meaning, formal expulsion will still occur as if the member were present). If we learn that a recently expelled member (or one who is fleeing our disciplinary action) is seeking membership with another church, one of our elders will, in most cases, attempt to arrange a private meeting with a pastor of that church along with the offender, in order to discuss the ongoing offense and protect the other church from harm (2 Timothy 4:14-15).

7. Where two members disagree regarding blame or degrees of responsibility, the matter should be brought before the elders and/or other mature men in the church who will judge according to the pattern found in 1 Corinthians 6:1-8.

8. Every member must agree that he or she will never initiate, pursue, or participate in any civil legal action against the church or against any member in connection with a disciplinary matter (see *The Fellowship of the Spirit*). In fact, any Christian considering civil legal action against another Christian for any reason should consider Paul's prohibition of such behavior (1 Corinthians 6:1-8).

9. Persistent and willful non-attendance is a sin requiring church discipline (Hebrews 10:24-25). Except where persistent non-attendance is the result of unavoidable circumstances (e.g. extended illness, incapacitation, out-of-town college education, military service, etc.), it will be considered a public offense and addressed appropriately. Those who persist in their non-attendance without legitimate excuse, even after exhortations and warnings from the church, will be expelled from membership. (Note: We have established no specific length of time to designate non-attendance as "persistent." Each situation will be treated as unique. Also, we will be diligent in conducting the most thorough and comprehensive investigation possible in determining the reason(s) for non-attendance. We will assume, until conclusive proof to the contrary exists, that the reason(s) are legitimate. Only when we are certain that the offender is *willfully* and *sinfully* neglecting the church will he be disciplined and/or expelled.)

10. Paul's words in 1 Timothy 5:19 ("Do not receive an accusation against an elder except from two or three witnesses.") should not be construed to mean that elders are to be protected from proper disciplinary action. Paul knew that elders, being in a position of authority, could easily become the objects of false or frivolous accusations. His command is simply a warning to watch for such abuses. Elders are church members just as all others, and are subject to discipline according to the same biblical principles as previously stated. (Note: The removal of an elder from his position due to an evident lack of biblical qualification is an issue we have not addressed in detail in this statement. For this, see *Appointment and Removal of Elders* at *www.CCWonline.org.*)

11. The training and discipline of children is the responsibility and biblical obligation of parents, particularly fathers (Proverbs 13:24; 19:18; 23:13-14; Ephesians 6:4). Member-parents who refuse or neglect to properly train and discipline a child, resulting in the perpetuation of sinful behavior on the part of the child, are committing a public offense and are subject to church discipline. In the event that an older child has become a member, yet is living under parental authority, the parent(s) remain responsible. If the member-parent(s) of a member-child refuse or neglect to train and/or discipline, resulting in the perpetuation of the child's sinful behavior, both the member-parent(s) and the member-child are subject to the discipline of the church. This is not meant to refer to parents who *do* properly, diligently, and biblically train and discipline a particularly obstinate child who nevertheless remains rebellious and disobedient. Even in these rare cases, however, whether the child is a member or not, if his or her behavior is so disruptive, immoral, and/or violent that the meetings of the church cannot proceed in a safe, peaceful, and orderly manner, he or she will be excluded from attendance or expelled from membership.

Final Thoughts on Church Discipline

There is admittedly a certain tension between the different principles involved in church discipline. On the one hand there is the gentleness of Galatians 6:1, on the other, the severity of Titus 1:13. While we may never be judgmental in our attitudes (Matthew 7:1), we must nevertheless judge among ourselves (1 Corinthians 5:12). Just as we are called to love in a manner that is willing to overlook certain sins (1 Peter 4:8), we must also "exhort one another daily" so that none will be "hardened through the deceitfulness of sin" (Hebrews 3:13). The tension is seen most clearly in that we are to love our brother as Christ loved us (John 13:34-35), yet remain willing to consider him an unbeliever and cast him away if he continues in sin (Matthew 18:17; 1 Corinthians 5:11).

We might be tempted to use the word "balance" in describing our desire to manage this tension. But as it is all-too-commonly understood, "balance" means compromise—easing away from convictions and obligations in order not to appear unbalanced or overly zealous. The problem with this understanding is that Scripture never tells Christians to be "balanced" people in this way. On the contrary, we are told to be zealous and fervent, *both* in our love for one another (Colossians 3:14; 1 Peter 4:8), *and* in our pursuit of holiness and purity (Titus 2:14; Hebrews 12:14-17).

What this means for the church in the area of discipline is that we must never rely upon human understanding, which is prone to setting itself against the Word of God. It means we must trust, study, and obey the Scriptures, even when the perceived tension between biblical obligations seems unbearable. We must hold *both* goals of church discipline in the highest regard, always allowing the Word of God to determine our course of action.

---

[1] We are indebted here to Rev. Eleazer Savage who published a *Manual of Church Discipline* in 1845. It is difficult to find a complete copy of this work, but a helpful portion is published in the book, *Polity: Biblical Arguments on How to Conduct Church Life*, edited by Mark Dever, (Washington D.C.: Center for Church Reform, 2001.), pp. 479-523.

[2] In our wealthy and materialistic society, Christians often tend to trivialize covetousness, but this should never be. Covetousness is a serious sin—one that is utterly uncharacteristic of a true Christian if it becomes a pattern of life. A covetous person is one whose affections are not for God, but rather for worldly things. Instead of worshiping God and loving Him with all his heart, soul, mind, and strength, the covetous person has an inordinate craving for money, material goods, or the lusts of the flesh. Paul refers to covetousness as idolatry (Col. 3:5). He lists it as one of a number of sins that are bringing the wrath of God "upon the sons of disobedience" (Col. 3:6). Concerning the love (or coveting) of money, Paul told Timothy that it was "a root of all kinds of evil" (1 Tim. 6:10). And John was speaking of covetousness when he wrote, "Do not love the world or the things in the world. If anyone loves the world, the love of the Father is not in him" (1 John 2:15). "Do not be deceived," Paul wrote to the church at Corinth. No covetous person "will inherit the kingdom of God" (1 Cor. 6:9-10).

Key Passages of Scripture Regarding Church Discipline

Pursue peace with all people, and holiness, without which no one will see the Lord: looking carefully lest anyone fall short of the grace of God; lest any root of bitterness springing up cause trouble, and by this many become defiled; lest there be any fornicator or profane person like Esau, who for one morsel of food sold his birthright.

Hebrews 12:14-16

And have no fellowship with the unfruitful works of darkness, but rather expose them.

Ephesians 5:11

Moreover if your brother sins against you, go and tell him his fault between you and him alone. If he hears you, you have gained your brother. But if he will not hear, take with you one or two more, that 'by the mouth of two or three witnesses every word may be established.' And if he refuses to hear them, tell it to the church. But if he refuses even to hear the church, let him be to you like a heathen and a tax collector.

Matthew 18:15-17

It is actually reported that there is sexual immorality among you, and such sexual immorality as is not even named among the Gentiles—that a man has his father's wife. And you are puffed up and have not rather mourned, that he who has done this deed might be taken away from among you. . . . deliver such a one to Satan for the destruction of the flesh, that his spirit may be saved in the day of the Lord Jesus. . . . Your glorying is not good. Do you not know that a little leaven leavens the whole lump? Therefore purge out the old leaven . . . I have written to you not to keep company with anyone named a brother, who is sexually immoral, or coveteous, or an idolater, or a reviler, or a drunkard, or an extortioner—not even to eat with such a person. . . . For what have I to do with judging those also who are outside? Do you not judge those who are inside? But those who are outside God judges. Therefore 'put away from yourselves the evil person.'

1 Corinthians 5:1,2,5-7,11-13

Brethren, if a man is overtaken in any trespass, you who are spiritual restore such a one in a spirit of gentleness, considering yourself lest you also be tempted. Bear one another's burdens and so fulfill the law of Christ.

Galatians 6:1-2

Brethren, if anyone among you wanders from the truth, and someone turns him back, let him know that he who turns a sinner from the error of his way will save a soul from death and cover a multitude of sins.

James 5:19-20

Now we exhort you, brethren, warn those who are unruly . . .

1 Thessalonians 5:14

But we command you, brethren, in the name of our Lord Jesus Christ, that you withdraw from every brother who walks disorderly and not according to the tradition which he received from us. . . . And if anyone does not obey our word in this epistle, note that person and do not keep company with him, that he may be ashamed. Yet do not count him as an enemy, but admonish him as a brother.

2 Thessalonians 3:6,14-15

Those who are sinning rebuke in the presence of all, that the rest also may fear.

1 Timothy 5:20

Open rebuke is better than love carefully concealed.

Proverbs 27:5

Reject a divisive man after the first and second admonition, knowing that such a person is warped and sinning, being self-condemned.

Titus 3:10-11

Now I urge you, brethren, note those who cause divisions and offenses, contrary to the doctrine which you learned, and avoid them.

Romans 16:17

Whoever transgresses and does not abide in the doctrine of Christ does not have God. . . . If anyone comes to you and does not bring this doctrine, do not receive him into your house nor greet him; for he who greets him shares in his evil deeds.

2 John 9-11

Now I rejoice, not that you were made sorry, but that your sorrow led to repentance. For you were made sorry in a godly manner . . . For godly sorrow produces repentance leading to salvation, not to be regretted; but the sorrow of the world produces death. For observe this very thing, that you sorrowed in a godly manner: What diligence it produced in you, what clearing of yourselves, what indignation, what fear, what vehement desire, what zeal, what vindication! In all these things you proved yourselves to be clear in this matter.

2 Corinthians 7:9-11

Acknowledgements

The documents in this book were written by Jim Elliff and Daryl Wingerd, founding pastors of Christ Fellowship of Kansas City. They were assisted in great measure by some of the men of Christ Fellowship, particularly in the process of reviewing the Scripture proofs for the statement of faith, as well as discussing and refining the discipline statement.

While these documents were prepared primarily with Christ Fellowship in mind, the statement of faith (*Holding Fast the Word of Life*) and the membership agreement (*The Fellowship of the Spirit*) were soon adopted for use by other churches. The discipline statement (*Restoring Those Who Fall*) was then reviewed by Dr. Jay Adams and included in an issue of his *Journal of Modern Ministry*. This use of the documents outside of Christ Fellowship seemed to indicate a present need in the modern church for solid, foundational materials in the areas of doctrine and church polity. Therefore, it was decided that they should be published in this form and made available for wider use. It is hoped that by God's grace, they will continue to be found helpful as others seek to build, strengthen, or reform local churches.

These documents may be adopted in their present form by simply using this book as a brief manual of polity and a statement of doctrinal convictions.

If minor alterations are needed to reflect the specific beliefs and/or practices of your church, changes and/or additions may be typed and affixed either inside the front cover, or in the blank pages at the end of the book.

Each of the documents in this book may also be found online at *www.ChristFellowshipKC.org*. If the online documents are used, we request that the full copyright information be included. If adaptations are deemed necessary for use in your church, please contact us by e-mail at *MinistryCenter@ChristFellowshipKC.org* for copyright instructions.